THE
STATUE
OF
LIBERTY

WILLIAM E.
SHAPIRO

THE
STATUE
OF
LIBERTY

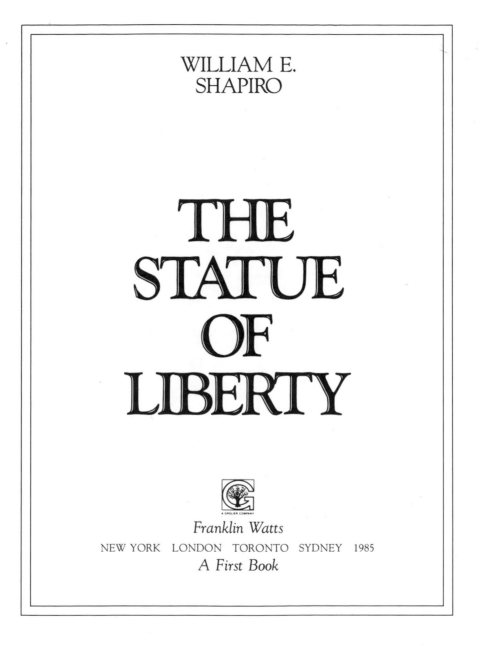

Franklin Watts

NEW YORK   LONDON   TORONTO   SYDNEY   1985

A First Book

Cover photograph courtesy of Shostal Associates

Photographs courtesy of
National Park Service: Statue of Liberty,
N.M./American Museum of Immigration.

Library of Congress Cataloging in Publication Data

Shapiro, William E.
The Statue of Liberty.

(A First book)
Includes index.
Summary: Describes the conception and building of the
giant statue known as Miss Liberty, its erection on
Bedloe's Island, and the efforts in this century to
modernize and renovate the monument.
1. Statue of Liberty (New York, N.Y.)—Juvenile
literature. 2. Statue of Liberty National Monument
(New York, N.Y.)—Juvenile literature. 3. New York
(N.Y.)—Statues—Juvenile literature. [1. Statue of
Liberty National Monument (New York, N.Y.)] I. Title.
F128.64.L6S49 1985   974.7′1   85-8893
ISBN 0-531-10047-2

CONTENTS

CHAPTER ONE

THE SYMBOL OF AMERICA

I will never forget the joy I felt when I saw . . . the Statue of Liberty after so many dark days on board the crowded ship. There was the symbol of all my dreams—freedom to start out in a new life." The immigrant who voiced these words did not speak for himself alone. He spoke for the millions of other immigrants who made the difficult and sometimes dangerous journey from the Old World to the New. To them America was the land of liberty. It was the land of opportunity. It was the land where anything was possible. It was the land of hope. And the Statue of Liberty was the symbol of that hope.

The Statue of Liberty was erected on Bedloe's Island (now Liberty Island) in 1886. Before that, the flow of immigrants to the United States was a steady stream. Now, in the latter part of the nineteenth century, it became a torrent. In 1892 Ellis Island, which lies just north of the Statue of Liberty in Upper New York Bay, was made the nation's major processing center for immigrants. There were no planes then, so immigrants passing through Ellis Island came by ship. And to get to Ellis Island the ships had to pass by Liberty. She was the first thing these immigrants saw in their new homeland.

What did these people see? They saw the majestic figure of a woman towering 151 feet (46 m) into the air. But she seemed even taller than that, for she stood on a pedestal and base which raised her up another 154 feet (47 m). They saw a face that radiated strength and wisdom and hope; and this gave them hope. They saw her standing alone—confidently—on an island; and this gave them confidence. They saw her hold high the torch of liberty; and this made them feel free.

During the first decade of this century, nearly nine million people left their homelands for America. Nearly two thousand five hundred of them went through Ellis Island every day. If any of these new Americans had visited the Statue of Liberty in 1903 or later—and no doubt many of them did—they would have seen a bronze plaque on one of the inner walls of the pedestal. Inscribed on the plaque was a poem, "The New Colossus," written in 1883 by Emma Lazarus. The last five lines of this poem are an eloquent plea by Lady Liberty. No other words so beautifully express the meaning of this beacon of hope.

"Give me your tired, your poor,
Your huddled masses yearning to breathe free,
The wretched refuse of your teeming shore,
Send these, the homeless, tempest-tost to me,
I lift my lamp beside the golden door!"

A young man named Edward Corsi was one of those "homeless, tempest-tost" immigrants. "I looked at the statue," he wrote,

Immigrants passing the Statue of
Liberty on the way to Ellis Island

[3]

"with a sense of bewilderment, half doubting its reality. Looming shadowy through the mist, it brought silence to the decks of the *Florida*. This symbol of America—this enormous expression of what we had all been taught was the inner meaning of this new country we were coming to—inspired awe in the hopeful immigrants." Edward Corsi, in later years, became commissioner of the Ellis Island Immigrant Processing Center.

Immigrants still flock to America, though their numbers are not as great as they were early in this century. And most of them probably fly in or come across the nation's border with Mexico. As a result, few of them see the Statue of Liberty as they arrive, as did the immigrants of years ago. But the power of the statue's symbolism remains.

LAND OF REFUGE

Auguste Bartholdi created the statue as a symbol of liberty. It later became the symbolic Mother of Exiles. Today, probably more than anything else, the statue symbolizes what's best about the United States.

What *is* best about America? Why did one German poet write, "America, in every latitude you are the true land of refuge. Wherever people struggle, to whom do they stretch their hand?"

America *has* been a place of refuge ever since the first colonies were established at Jamestown and Plymouth in the early 1600s. The founding of the nation was accompanied by an amazing document—the Declaration of Independence. It proposed that all men—all people—are created equal, and that they have the right to "Life, Liberty and the pursuit of Happiness." And when the United States Constitution was written, the Bill of Rights guaranteed the American people freedom of

The Statue of Liberty

religion, press, speech, and assembly. These were revolutionary ideas for the world of 1776. Two hundred years ago, no other nation made such guarantees to its people.

Even a hundred years ago, when the Statue of Liberty was placed on its pedestal in New York Harbor, most of the peoples of the world had few rights. Much of Europe was ruled by kings and czars and emperors, and the people had little or no say about who governed them or how they were governed. Some, however, hoped that the American form of democracy would spread to other nations. Two of these people were Édouard-Réné Lefebvre de Laboulaye and Auguste Bartholdi. These two men of France both felt, as the American essayist E. B. White would write decades later, that "Liberty . . . spreads wherever it can capture the imagination of men." They felt, too, that a Statue of Liberty would help spread the ideal of liberty throughout the world.

CHAPTER
TWO

A MONUMENT
FOR
AMERICA

F rédéric Auguste Bartholdi, creator of the Statue
of Liberty, was born on August 2, 1834, in the city of Colmar,
France. Colmar is in northeastern France, in the province of
Alsace. It is not far from the Rhine River, which forms the
boundary between France and Germany. The Bartholdis had
settled in Colmar nearly two hundred years before the birth of
Auguste (he never used his first name, Frédéric). But they probably came originally from Italy. Auguste's father, a civil servant
who owned some land in Colmar, died when Auguste was only
two years old. Auguste's mother, Charlotte, then moved to Paris
with Auguste and his older brother, Charles. She felt that the
schools in Paris were better than those in Colmar.

Young Auguste was not that good a student, but the one
subject he truly loved was art. He liked to paint and draw, and
he was quite good at this. During his teens, Auguste discovered
that he was even better at sculpting. Others soon noticed his
talents. When Auguste was only eighteen years old, he was commissioned to sculpt a statue of General Jean Rapp. During the
Napoleonic Wars of the early 1800s, Rapp had been one of

Napoleon's best commanders. Rapp, like Bartholdi, had been born in Colmar.

When he was twenty-two years old, Bartholdi completed the statue of General Rapp. The statue was 12 feet (3.6 m) tall, and when placed on its pedestal it towered 26 feet (7.8 m) above the street. Bartholdi's first statue was big. But many years later he would sculpt even larger ones. One of these, a lion made out of granite, was 38 feet (11.6 m) high. But Bartholdi had even grander ideas.

EGYPTIAN TRAVELS

In 1856 Bartholdi traveled with a friend to Egypt. There he saw the massive pyramids and the Great Sphinx at Giza. The Sphinx, a monumental sculpture with the head of a king and the body of a lion, is 66 feet (20 m) high and 240 feet (73 m) long. One of the pyramids Bartholdi saw was almost 500 feet (152 m) high.

At the time of Bartholdi's visit to Egypt, Ferdinand de Lesseps, a French engineer, was planning to build the Suez Canal. This waterway would link the Red Sea and the Mediterranean Sea. It would enable ships to sail from Europe to Asia without making the long and difficult trip around the southern tip of Africa. De Lesseps completed the Suez Canal in 1869. Bartholdi went to Egypt once again, to attend the opening ceremonies. While there, he thought about building a giant statue that would serve as a lighthouse in the canal. He wanted to make the statue in the form of a woman clothed in a flowing toga and holding a giant beacon.

Frédéric Auguste Bartholdi

In the 1860s Egypt was becoming modernized. Bartholdi felt that the statue would symbolize the Western world's helping the Eastern world in its quest for modernization. He made many sketches of the proposed statue, but he could find no one to support the project. Bartholdi was very disappointed, of course, but now he had another project in mind, one that would use some of the same features he had envisioned for the Suez lighthouse.

AN IDEA IS BORN

Four years earlier, in 1865, Bartholdi had attended a dinner at the home of Édouard-Réné Lefebvre de Laboulaye. Laboulaye, a legal scholar, teacher, and historian, lived near Versailles and frequently invited a number of people to his home for dinner parties. At these parties they would discuss world affairs and the political situation in France. Laboulaye especially admired the United States. He thought that it had a very good system of government. He also thought the people of America enjoyed freedoms that no other peoples in the world had. Laboulaye had many well-known friends in the United States, and he had written several books about the country.

Laboulaye, Bartholdi, and the other guests discussed the end of the American Civil War and the assassination of Lincoln. They also talked about the friendship that existed between France and the United States. This friendship had existed ever since the American War of Independence which began in 1776. One of France's great military leaders, the Marquis de Lafayette, had helped the struggling American colonies gain their independence from England.

"The two nations have mutual ideals," Laboulaye told his friends. "If a monument were to be built in America as a memorial to their independence," he went on, "I should think it very natural if it were built by united efforts, if it were a common work of both nations."

Bartholdi listened, and he began to think about building the memorial to American independence. But many years would pass before he would be able to begin his work. For one thing, Napoleon III, the autocratic ruler of France, would never allow a Frenchman to build a monument for the United States. Napoleon disliked the United States because it stood for democracy and freedom. He did not want the French people thinking too much about democracy and freedom. Napoleon had even hoped that the Confederacy would win the Civil War and that the Union would fall apart.

WAR

In July 1870, France found itself in a very bitter and destructive war with Prussia and the other German states. (The German states did not form a single, unified nation until 1871.) The war lasted less than a year. France, which had old military equipment and inept generals, was soundly beaten.

When the war started, Bartholdi enlisted in the French National Guard. He was made a major. When he heard that the Germans were threatening Colmar, where his mother was living, he asked to be sent there to organize the city's defenses. He was given permission to do this, but when he got to Colmar, he found very few men willing to defend the city. And when a force of five thousand German soldiers prepared an attack on the city, Bartholdi's force dwindled to less than twenty. The situation was hopeless, Bartholdi knew, so he gave up the fight. He was unhappy about this, but he knew there was nothing he could do.

The French soon suffered even greater defeats. When Paris was besieged, they were forced to surrender. For France, there was only one positive result of the Franco-Prussian War: Napoleon III was ousted. He went into exile in England, where he died a few years later. The people of France were now able to turn their attention to establishing a democratic form of government.

AMERICAN TRAVELS

Laboulaye believed the time was now right to begin work on the monument for the United States. France had returned to the path of democracy. And in a few years, in 1876, the United States would celebrate the one hundredth anniversary of the signing of the Declaration of Independence. A suitable monument, Laboulaye believed, would forge strong ties between the United States and France. As a result, he urged Bartholdi to visit the United States and learn all he could about the country and its people. By doing this, Bartholdi would be able to create a meaningful monument. "Propose to our friends over there," he told Bartholdi, "that together we make a monument in remembrance of the ancient friendship of France and the United States."

Bartholdi could hardly contain his excitement about the trip. He hurriedly booked passage on the steamship *Pereire*. During the voyage he made a number of sketches of his proposed statue. But he was not happy with any of them. His ship entered New York harbor on June 21, 1871, after a thirteen-day voyage. There he saw Bedloe's Island. He knew immediately that this island would make the perfect setting for a monument to liberty.

Bedloe's Island is in Upper New York Bay. It is very small—only 12 acres (4.8 ha). But Bartholdi saw that every ship

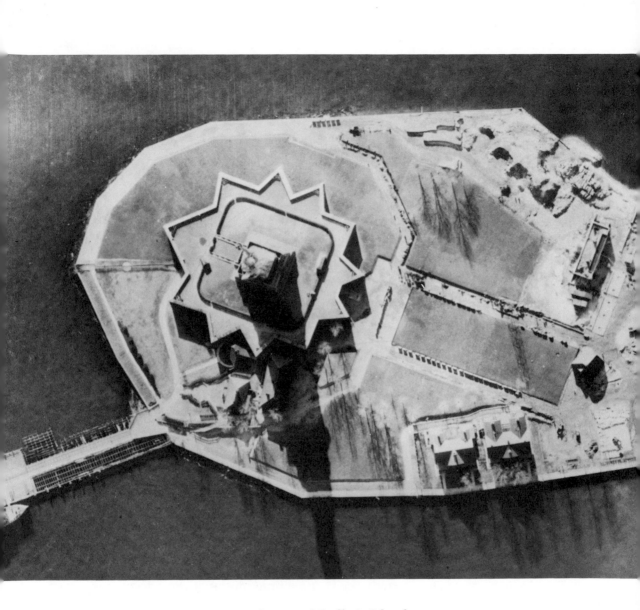

Aerial view of Bedloe's Island
before the Statue was built.
The star-shaped structure is Fort Wood.

entering New York Harbor would have to pass by Bedloe's Island. And everyone on those ships would see a statue there. Now all he had to do was convince the Americans that they should join in the project.

Thrilled by his discovery of Bedloe's Island as the perfect site for the statue, Bartholdi began sketching once again. This time he was successful. The sketches, in fact, looked similar in some ways to the sketches he had made of the Egyptian peasant woman for his proposed lighthouse in the Suez Canal. Bartholdi thought that he would call his American statue Liberty Enlightening the World.

Bartholdi's stay in the United States was an eye-opener for him. With his keen mind, he began to understand the American people. He was able to see more clearly the national character of the people he had long admired. And the more he saw, the more he was certain that he would somehow build his statue.

With letters of introduction from Laboulaye, Bartholdi met many prominent and influential people. He met the artist John La Farge and the poet Henry Wadsworth Longfellow. He met Senator Charles Sumner of Massachusetts. He even met President Ulysses S. Grant. But when Bartholdi told Grant of his plans for a monument to American independence, Grant showed little enthusiasm.

Bartholdi also met the architect Richard Morris Hunt. Hunt, who had studied architecture in Paris, was well known for building beautiful mansions for the rich in New York City and in Newport, Rhode Island. Bartholdi told Hunt all about his plans for Liberty Enlightening the World. He didn't know it then, but many years later Hunt would design the pedestal for Liberty.

Bartholdi stayed in the East for about two months. Then he began a trip across the United States by train. The nation's first transcontinental railway line had been completed only two years earlier. From New York State, Bartholdi traveled west to Detroit, Chicago, Omaha, Salt Lake City, and San Francisco. On the return trip, he stopped at St. Louis and Cincinnati. He ended his trip in the nation's capital, Washington, D.C. Everything he had seen impressed him—especially the size of the country. "Everything in America is so big," he wrote Laboulaye. "Here, even the peas are big."

Now that he had seen much of the country, Bartholdi was convinced that the American people would be enthusiastic about his Liberty Enlightening the World. But this was not the case—at least not then. No one offered to give money for the project—not wealthy individuals and not the American government. Still, Bartholdi was optimistic when he returned to France.

FROM LIONS TO LIBERTY

Despite his optimism, Bartholdi did not start to work on his project when he returned to his studio. For one thing, he had no money. As a result, he began working on other projects. One of these was the Lion of Belfort, the giant granite statue mentioned earlier. But even while working on other projects, Bartholdi found time to improve his design of Liberty Enlightening the World. He sculpted a number of small models. The first Lady Liberty held the torch in her left hand.

In 1873 Bartholdi was commissioned to sculpt a statue of the Marquis de Lafayette. Just as Lafayette had helped the Americans during the Revolutionary War, many Americans had helped France during the Franco-Prussian War. They had given moral support, and they had given money. As a result, the French wanted to thank the American people by presenting them with a statue of Lafayette.

Bartholdi completed the statue of Lafayette in time for the

American centennial celebrations in 1876. It was unveiled in New York City's Union Square. Bartholdi and Laboulaye had also hoped to complete Liberty Enlightening the World in time for the centennial celebrations. But fund raising for the statue did not even begin until the fall of 1875. A year earlier, Laboulaye had set up the Franco-American Union. Its task was to oversee the completion of the statue.

Much of the money for the statue came from the schoolchildren of France. By the end of 1875 enough money had been raised for Bartholdi to start work. But this money was to be used only for the statue itself. Laboulaye felt that the American people should pay for the pedestal on which the statue would stand. In this way, it would be a project shared by the two nations.

Bartholdi set up a special studio at Gaget, Gauthier and Company in Paris. This company had a staff of outstanding craftsmen. Some of them had worked on the spires of Notre Dame Cathedral. Others were experienced copper workers. Bartholdi met with the craftsmen and described the statue he wanted to build. He showed them the 4-foot (1.2-m) clay model he had constructed. And he told them that the statue would be made of copper, not stone or bronze, which would be too heavy.

By this time, Bartholdi had refined his plans for the statue. Liberty would be in the form of a woman dressed in a Roman-type robe and sandals. Her face would be serene yet strong, compassionate yet courageous. She would be a maternal figure offering shelter and welcome to those in need. Indeed, Bartholdi's

Bartholdi's statue of Lafayette
in Union Square, New York City

own mother was the model for Liberty's face. And a young woman whom Bartholdi would later marry, Jeanne-Emilie Baheux de Puysieux, served as the model for the statue's arms.

The right arm, raised high in the air, firmly held the torch of liberty. And atop Liberty's massive head, Bartholdi had placed a tiara with seven spikes. These represented the world's seven oceans and seven continents. In her left hand, Liberty held a tablet. On it was inscribed "July IV, MDCCLXXVI" (July 4, 1776)—the date of the signing of the Declaration of Independence. And at her feet, where the flowing robe met the pedestal, Bartholdi placed a broken chain. To the sculptor, this represented Liberty's breaking free from bondage.

Thus, as 1875 ended, Bartholdi knew that his and Laboulaye's plans, now ten years in the making, would come to fruition. No longer was there any doubt in his mind.

Bartholdi's Paris studio

CHAPTER THREE

THE BUILDING OF LIBERTY

artholdi's Baby!" yelled some American critics of Liberty Enlightening the World. "Frenchman's Folly!" cried others. Even *The New York Times* belittled Bartholdi's ideas. And in general, the American people showed very little interest. Yet here it was, the beginning of 1876, and these people were well along with their plans to celebrate in July the centennial of the signing of the Declaration of Independence. Why, Bartholdi wondered, didn't they see the connection between the centennial and Liberty? Why didn't they see that Liberty would be the everlasting symbol of American independence and freedom? Why didn't they see, as Laboulaye had said, that "This Liberty . . . will be the American Liberty [who holds] a beacon which enlightens."

Bartholdi had wanted to complete the statue in 1876, so that it would be in America during the centennial celebrations. But now he saw that this would be impossible. He planned, instead, to send just the right arm and the torch. These could be completed on time. He would send them to the Philadelphia Centennial Exposition for the Fourth of July celebrations there.

Bartholdi also planned to make a second trip to the United States. He would be part of the French delegation to the centennial celebrations. In April he attended a benefit performance at the Paris Opera whose purpose was to raise more money for the statue. The French composer Charles Gounod wrote a special Liberty Cantata for this event. It started off with the words, "I have triumphed! I am one hundred years old! My name is Liberty!" This benefit did not raise a lot of money for the statue. But Bartholdi was pleased by the coverage given by the French newspapers. When he began his second trip to America in May, he was very optimistic. But then, Bartholdi was always optimistic.

THE SECOND AMERICAN TRIP

He remained optimistic even when he arrived in New York City and found that his statue of Lafayette, which had been in America for months, was still in its crate. The Americans had not even built the pedestal on which it would stand. So with his usual energy, Bartholdi traveled around and spoke to people and helped raise money for the pedestal.

Bartholdi also visited Bedloe's Island. On the island was Fort Wood, which was named after a hero of the War of 1812. The walls of the fort were in the shape of an eleven-pointed star. Bartholdi knew that this statue should be erected in the center of the star. But he now wanted to determine which way Liberty should face. At first he thought she should face south; then people on ships coming from the Atlantic Ocean to New York City's piers would look directly at Liberty's face as the ships traveled north.

But Bartholdi changed his mind about this. He had a better idea. He would have her face south by southeast. He did this for three reasons. First, if she faced south by southeast, her back would not be to New York City. Second, people on ships coming up the harbor would be able to see Liberty's face for a longer period of time. And third, as Bartholdi explained it, "to those coming to America, Liberty would appear to be facing due east to the Old World," to their old homelands.

Satisfied with this decision, Bartholdi traveled on to Philadelphia for the centennial celebrations. There he saw an enormous fountain that he had designed for the centennial. But Liberty's arm and torch, still incomplete, would not arrive in Philadelphia until the fall. When the arm and torch did arrive, many people wanted the entire Statue of Liberty to be located there—the Birthplace of the United States—if New York City, for some reason, turned it down.

Bartholdi, of course, was determined that the statue would be on Bedloe's Island, which he was already calling Liberty Island. New York City, the gateway to America, was the only proper location for Liberty, Bartholdi frequently commented. Bartholdi returned to New York City for the unveiling of his statue of Lafayette. The pedestal was finally completed. The statue had been on display in Central Park, and now it was moved to Union Square, its permanent home.

Many newspapers reported the unveiling of the statue of Lafayette. There were stories about Bartholdi and about the gift of his Liberty Enlightening the World to the American people. This helped tremendously in the fund-raising effort.

But once again *The New York Times* attacked the project. It said that the arm and torch on display at the Philadelphia Cen-

*Arm and torch of Ms. Liberty
on display at 1876 International
Exposition in Philadelphia*

tennial Exposition had cost $200,000, and that the entire statue and pedestal would cost more than $40 million. This was not true, and Bartholdi was very upset by the newspaper article. He was even more upset when some people said that he would make a fortune by building the Statue of Liberty. This was also untrue: Bartholdi had even paid for his two trips to the United States. He never asked the Franco-American Union to pay him back. He did not care about money. He only cared about building Liberty and seeing it placed in New York Harbor, where it would "enlighten the world."

During this trip to America, Bartholdi once again visited the artist John La Farge. It was at La Farge's home that Bartholdi married Jeanne-Emilie Baheux de Puysieux. With his new wife, Bartholdi returned to New York City, where he met the artist Edward Moran, who had painted "Liberty Lighting the World's Commerce." This beautiful painting showed Liberty on her island surrounded by a flotilla of large and small boats, all flying French and American flags. Moran had given a lot of money to the French victims of the Franco-Prussian War. Now he displayed his new painting of Liberty at many fund-raising events. Still, not enough money was coming in. Bartholdi told his American supporters that they would have to raise the money for the pedestal and foundation. One of those he spoke to was William M. Evarts, a lawyer and a politician. He formed the American Committee for the Statue of Liberty, whose job it would be to raise money for the pedestal and foundation.

Bartholdi returned to Paris in January 1877. His trip to the United States had been very successful. He had married a woman he loved very much. He had finally seen his statue of Lafayette put in place in New York's Union Square. He had seen his beautiful fountain at the Philadelphia Centennial Exposition. He had shown the American people the beauty of Liberty's arm and torch. And, most important, he had seen that many more Americans now supported him and his project. They had even formed a group to raise funds for the pedestal and foundation for the statue.

Soon after his return to France, Bartholdi learned that the United States Congress had voted to accept the Statue of Liberty from France. Unfortunately, Congress did not approve any money for the project. But this did not upset Bartholdi. He felt that the moral support given to him by the Congress was as important as money.

So Bartholdi's trip to America had been important and successful for a number of reasons. Now he returned to his work on the statue.

BUILDING THE STATUE

How did Bartholdi make this statue? First he made a clay model just over 4 feet (1.2 m) in height. He then made a model that was 9 feet (2.7 m) tall and then one that was 36 feet (11 m) tall. Both of these were made of plaster. On the 36-foot (11-m) model the workers placed a great many small points, or dots. The distance between each dot was measured and multiplied four times. This gave the dimensions for the completed statue. Each part of the model—the face, the body, the feet—was marked with these dots, then measured and multiplied four times.

The points, now in full scale, were connected with strips of wood. These strips of wood formed a wooden frame. Plaster was placed over the wooden frame to form a mold. Finally, a wooden mold was placed over the plaster mold. The copper work was ready to begin.

Bartholdi used a copper-working method called repoussé. With this method, the copper is molded from the inside. There were three hundred pieces of copper. Each was placed over a part of the mold and hammered or beaten into shape. Bartholdi now had three hundred pieces of copper which, when put together, would be the "Copper Lady." Bartholdi had already sculpted a statue using this technique. It was a statue of Vercingetorix, a French hero who had fought against the conquering Roman legions before the time of Christ and who was executed by Caesar in 52 B.C. Bartholdi's statue of Vercingetorix stood 23 feet (7 m) high.

So Bartholdi now had the skin of his statue. The copper was only $3/32$ of an inch (0.24 cm) thick. Yet when it was assembled it would be over 151 feet (46 m) high. The head alone would be more than 17 feet (5.2 m) from chin to crown. The mouth would be 3 feet (0.9 m) wide, and each eye would be 2.5 feet (0.76 m). The index finger would be 8 feet (2.4 m) long and its fingernail would cover almost a square foot (0.093 sq. m) in area. Liberty would be 35 feet (10.7 m) thick at her waist, and her right arm would be 42 feet (12.8 m) long. How would this massive statue be supported? How would Bartholdi keep 100 tons (91 MT) of copper standing erect?

Fortunately for Bartholdi, there lived in France a great engineer named Alexandre Gustave Eiffel. Eiffel had built many bridges, including railroad bridges that Bartholdi himself had traveled over. In 1889 he would build the famous Paris landmark, the Eiffel Tower. Bartholdi asked Eiffel to design and construct a supporting framework for his Liberty Enlightening the World.

For the main, center support, Eiffel built a pylon nearly 100 feet (30 m) tall. Smaller spans of steel extended from this central support. These spans conformed to the shape of the statue. For the right arm and torch, Eiffel built a smaller network

The Statue outside Bartholdi's studio

of girders. Eiffel's work on the support system and Bartholdi's work on the copper skin went on at the same time. As each support section was completed, more of the copper skin was affixed to it. Outside of Bartholdi's studio, the people of Paris could watch as Lady Liberty grew foot by foot.

The arm and the torch were completed first. As mentioned earlier, these had been displayed at the Philadelphia Centennial Exposition in 1876. Visitors to the exposition could pay fifty cents for the privilege of climbing up into the torch. Two years later Bartholdi put the upper torso and head on display at the Paris Universal Exhibition.

Work moved ahead rather slowly at times, and Édouard de Laboulaye, who died during the winter of 1883–84, did not see his dream completely fulfilled. But Liberty was completed soon after his death. On July 4, 1884, on the street outside of Bartholdi's studio, the Statue of Liberty was officially presented to the United States. Ferdinand de Lesseps, builder of the Suez Canal, had taken Laboulaye's place as head of the Franco-American Union. He presented the Statue of Liberty to Levi P. Morton, the American ambassador to France. "We commit the Statue of Liberty to your care," he said, "that it may remain forever the pledge of bonds which shall unite France and the great American nation."

Lady Liberty was ready—ready to be shipped to her home in the United States. But the United States was not ready for her!

The foundation for the pedestal had been constructed by General Charles P. Stone, an engineer. The pedestal had been designed by Richard Morris Hunt, and a ferry, the *Bartholdi*, carried supplies to Bedloe's Island so that work could start on it. But little work was done because there was no money.

"If New York wants the Statue of Liberty, let the people of New York pay for it," cried too many people throughout the country. One New Yorker did try to do something. Joseph Pulitzer had come to the United States from Hungary. In 1883 he had bought *The World*, a daily newspaper, from millionaire Jay Gould. In an effort to get more people to read his newspaper, Pulitzer began a campaign to raise money to build the pedestal for the Statue of Liberty. He was only partially successful. The American Committee for the Statue of Liberty needed about $100,000 to complete the pedestal. The Committee appealed to the American people: "If the money is not now forthcoming the statue must return to its donors, to the everlasting disgrace of the American people . . . we ask you once and for all to prevent so painful and humiliating a catastrophe!"

CHAPTER FOUR

LIBERTY COMES TO AMERICA

O n a cold New Year's Day in 1885, the Statue of Liberty still stood in the courtyard of Gaget, Gauthier and Company in Paris. Despite the cold, Parisians by the thousands strolled by to glimpse the statue. Some climbed the 168 steps to the top. Others just admired Lady Liberty from the ground. As winter turned to spring, Bartholdi told his workmen to start dismantling the statue. It was time for it to be sent to America.

Copper sheet by copper sheet, bolt by bolt, Lady Liberty was taken apart. The steel framework, which looked as if it had been made from a giant erector set, was taken apart, too. Each piece was carefully marked with special code numbers, so that it would be easy to reassemble the statue in the United States. The 350 tons (317 MT) of copper and steel were then loaded onto a special train for the trip to Rouen, a river port on the Seine River about 70 miles (113 km) from Paris. Waiting at Rouen was the French Navy ship *Isère*. The 214 gigantic crates that contained the bits and pieces of the Statue were loaded onto the *Isère*. On May 21, 1885, she set sail for the United States.

Under normal weather conditions, the trip would have taken a little over a week. But almost as soon as the *Isère* left port she ran into a fierce storm. The ship was lashed by torrential rains and buffeted by gale-force winds. With her precious cargo, she finally reached New York on June 17. She was escorted into the harbor by ships of the French North Atlantic Naval Squadron. Other ships soon joined the naval parade to Bedloe's Island. There were at least a hundred ships of all shapes and sizes, many of them gaily decorated with French and American flags. As bands played, the sounds of "The Star Spangled Banner" and "La Marseillaise," the French national anthem, could be heard everywhere. Sometimes the sounds of booming cannons drowned out the music. Later, the *Isère*'s crewmen were paraded through the streets of New York. It was a day of joy in the city. It was a day of celebration. It was a day when Auguste Bartholdi felt especially proud. But it was also a day that might have been the most embarrassing one in American history. Joseph Pulitzer, publisher of *The World*, saved the American people from that.

LAST-MINUTE NEEDS

Editorials in his newspaper called on the people of America to give whatever they could afford—even pennies—so that the statue's pedestal could be completed. "Let us not wait for the millionaires to give this money," he wrote in March 1885. "It is not a gift from the millionaires of France to the millionaires of America, but a gift of the whole people of France to the whole people of America." Pulitzer promised to print in his newspaper the name of every person who donated money, however little.

This time the response was wonderful. From every corner of America, the money started to pour in. Children sent pennies and nickels. Their parents sent dollars. And when Pulitzer began to make fun of stingy millionaires of the day, they, too, began sending money.

On Tuesday, August 11, 1885, the headline of *The World* proclaimed, "ONE HUNDRED THOUSAND DOLLARS! TRIUMPHANT COMPLETION OF THE WORLD'S FUND FOR THE LIBERTY PEDESTAL." Accompanying this headline was a drawing of the Statue of Liberty. In Liberty's right hand she held not only the torch of liberty but the American flag. In her left hand she held a bag of money—enough to assure the completion of the pedestal. And on the pedestal was this inscription: "This pedestal to Liberty was provided by the voluntary contributions of 120,000 patriotic citizens of the American Union through the *New York World*." Pulitzer—and the American people—had saved the day.

The workers now rushed to complete the pedestal. It was in place by April 1886, and the complicated task of putting up Eiffel's steel skeleton began. This work took two months. In July the skeleton was firmly anchored to the pedestal. The crates containing the copper plates were then unpacked. At a special ceremony, the first piece of copper was riveted into place. Then another, and another. The first pieces of copper were given names. The first was called Bartholdi. Others were called Pulitzer and Eiffel and Hunt. But not every piece of copper was named, because there were three hundred of them. And more

Front page of The World, *August 11, 1885, announcing the attainment of Joseph Pulitzer's goal of raising $100,000, needed to build the Statue's pedestal*

0,220.   **The World.**   230,220
Circulation of THE SUNDAY WORLD   The Average Circulation of THE SUNDAY WORLD
of THE SUNDAY WORLD   is Larger than that of any other Newspaper Publi
hemisphere   on the Western Hemisphere.

ONE HUNDRED THOUSAND DOLLARS!

TRIUMPHANT COMPLETION OF THE WORLD'S FUND FOR THE LIBERTY PEDESTAL.

Story of the Greatest Popular Subscription Ever Raised in America—How the Republic Was Saved from Lasting Disgrace—An Event for Patriotic Citizens to Rejoice Over—A Roll of Honor Bearing the Names of 120,000 Generous Patriots—The Flags of France and the American Union Floating in Sisterly Sympathy—Over $2,500 Received Yesterday—The Grand Total Foots Up $102,006.39—A Generous Lady Pays $130 for the Washington Cent.

THIS PEDESTAL TO LIBERTY WAS PROVIDED BY THE VOLUNTARY CONTRIBUTIONS 120,000 PATRIOTIC CITIZENS OF THE AMERICAN UNION THROUGH THE NEW YORK WORLD FINS CORONAT OPUS

MURDERED IN HIS HOME.

A WEALTHY BROOKLYNITE SHOT DOWN BY A HIDDEN FOE.

Albert R. Herrick, Near Place of Business at No. 60 William Street, this City, Dies Before He Can Tell Who Fired the Fatal Shot—The Police Without a Clue.

The Resurrection of the Army.

WASHINGTON, Aug. 10.—The recent general army order sending officers back to their regiments after a period of four years on detached duty is provoking much discussion among officers in Washington.

Repairs at the White House.

WASHINGTON, Aug. 10.—The White House is now closed to visitors and will not be reopened until the President's return in September.

Forecasters Meet at Detroit.

DETROIT, Mich., Aug. 10.—The biennial meeting of the subsidiary high court of the Ancient Order of Foresters of the United States is now being held in this city.

Effect of Wisconsin High License.

MILWAUKEE, Wis., Aug. 10.—The new High License law of Wisconsin increasing the minimum rate of saloon license from $75 to $250 has now been in force three months and returns from some one hundred towns in the State show that the aggregate number of saloons has been diminished.

Return of Tuttle's Comet.

BOSTON, Aug. 9.—A minute message received at the Harvard College Observatory, from Kiel, Holstein, announces the discovery of Tuttle's comet.

Weather Indications.

Fair weather, a slight fall, followed by a slight rise in temperature.

than six hundred thousand rivets were used to attach them to the iron straps that held the copper skin of the statue to the steel skeleton.

THE DREAM COMES TRUE

Auguste Bartholdi arrived in the United States on October 25, 1886. With him were his wife and Ferdinand de Lesseps. "The dream of my life is accomplished," Bartholdi said. But his crowning moment would come three days later, on October 28, at the inaugural ceremonies for Liberty Enlightening the World.

When that day dawned, it was cold and rainy in New York City. But no one paid the least attention to the weather. This was Bartholdi Day. This was Liberty's Day. Twenty thousand policemen, firemen, soldiers, veterans, college students, and others marched in the largest parade New York City had ever seen. They made their way from Fifty-seventh Street and Fifth Avenue in Manhattan to the Battery at the very southern tip of Manhattan. Hundreds of thousands of people lined the parade route, cheering them on. Once again bands played the French and American national anthems. Guns were fired in salute.

The line of marchers made its way past Madison Square Park, where President Grover Cleveland and other important people sat in the reviewing stand. As the last of the marchers passed by, the president and his party hurried to the East River.

Facing: *Closeup of Statue's hand and torch*
Over left: *tablet*
Over right: *head*

Here they boarded boats for the choppy ride to Bedloe's Island. They headed south along Manhattan's east coast, and then sailed into the Upper Bay. Hundreds of ships were there before them, many of them bedecked with French and American flags. As the dignitaries looked up at Liberty, they saw that she, too, was wearing a French flag—around her face.

Bartholdi was already on Bedloe's Island. In fact, he was standing inside the crown. He would have the honor of removing the French flag by pulling on a rope. But first there were speeches to be made. One of the first to address the crowd was William Evarts, head of the American Committee for the Statue of Liberty. When Evarts paused during his speech, Bartholdi thought the speech was over. He pulled the rope, the flag fell, and Liberty's face, a beautiful copper color, was revealed. The crowd roared. Ships fired their guns and tooted their horns and blew their whistles. The scene was one of sheer joy and exuberance.

It took some time for the crowd to quiet down. Finally, President Cleveland spoke. "We will not forget that Liberty has made here her home," he said. "Nor shall her chosen altar be neglected . . . a stream of light shall pierce the darkness of ignorance and man's oppression until Liberty enlightens the world."

Later, when the lights in the torch were turned on as the sun was about to set, the torch was not as bright as Bartholdi had expected. But its symbolic glow would, indeed, "enlighten the world" for a century and more.

CHAPTER FIVE

ONE HUNDRED YEARS OF LADY LIBERTY

L iberty Island," Auguste Bartholdi said, "is destined to be made into a pleasure ground for the soul of the American people, a place of pilgrimage for citizens of the whole nation, a national museum of the glories and memories of the United States." If Bartholdi, who died in 1904, could somehow see the Statue of Liberty today, how thrilled he would be! His vision of Liberty Island has come to be. Nearly two million people take the short boat ride to the island every year. There they see Bartholdi's beautiful Liberty Enlightening the World. There they come to understand—and feel—her powerful symbolism. There they see statues of Bartholdi, Laboulaye, and Eiffel—the dreamers and the builders of the Statue of Liberty. There they see a statue of Pulitzer, who helped ensure that Liberty would have a resting place in America. There they see a statue of Emma Lazarus, whose forceful poem so movingly expresses the meaning of Liberty. And there they see the American Museum of Immigration, "a museum of the glories and memories of the United States." A visit to Liberty Island is a moving experience; for it has become, in Bartholdi's words, "a pleasure ground for the soul of the American people."

THE EARLY YEARS

But this was not how people saw the Statue of Liberty in its early years. It was certainly not how the government first saw it. Because Bartholdi's original conception of Liberty was as a light-house, the government placed it under the jurisdiction of the Government Light-House Board. It administered the statue from 1886 until 1902. But two other groups controlled other aspects of life on Liberty Island. A special civilian commission was responsible for the visitors to the island. And the United States Army controlled the military installation there—Fort Wood. President Theodore Roosevelt transferred jursidiction of the statue from the Light-House Board to the War Department in 1902.

By 1902, however, Liberty was witnessing the greatest influx of immigrants the United States had ever seen. Nearly 3.7 million immigrants entered the United States during the last decade of the nineteenth century. And in the first two decades of the twentieth century, the number of immigrants would swell to nearly 14.5 million. The Statue of Liberty was becoming the Mother of Exiles.

Perhaps in recognition of this, the War Department decided to engrave Emma Lazarus's poem "The New Colossus" on a bronze plaque and place the plaque on Liberty's pedestal. Her poem, like Liberty herself, was a symbol to these millions of immigrants.

> *Not like the brazen giant of Greek fame,*
> *With conquering limbs astride from land to land;*
> *Here at our sea-washed, sunset gates shall stand*
> *A mighty woman with a torch, whose flame*
> *Is the imprisoned lightning, and her name*
> *Mother of Exiles. From her beacon-hand*

Immigrants at Ellis Island

Glows world-wide welcome; her mild eyes command
The air-bridged harbor that twin cities frame.
"Keep, ancient lands, your storied pomp!" cries she
With silent lips. "Give me your tired, your poor,
Your huddled masses yearning to breathe free,
The wretched refuse of your teeming shore,
Send these, the homeless, tempest-tost to me,
I lift my lamp beside the golden door!"

Immigrants continued to pour into the United States even after World War I began in 1914. When the United States entered the war in 1917, the Statue of Liberty took on new meaning. It now became the symbol of the United States. Statue of Liberty posters appeared everywhere, and Liberty was on $15 billion worth of war bonds sold by the government. These Liberty Bonds helped finance the war effort.

While Liberty was helping the war effort, Pulitzer's newspaper, *The World*, was once again helping Liberty. Pulitzer had died in 1911, but the newspaper raised $30,000 to help modernize the statue. Floodlights were installed around the statue so that it could be seen at night, and hundreds of small pieces of copper were removed from the torch and replaced with amber glass. Brighter lights were then put in the torch. The torch was redesigned by Gutzon Borglum. Like Bartholdi, Borglum loved to work on giant sculptures. Later in his career, he would create the Mount Rushmore National Memorial. This huge carving in South Dakota shows the faces of four of America's greatest presidents: George Washington, Thomas Jefferson, Abraham Lincoln, and Theodore Roosevelt.

Emma Lazarus

In 1924 President Calvin Coolidge proclaimed the Statue of Liberty a national monument. In 1936 President Franklin D. Roosevelt presided over celebrations for the statue's fiftieth anniversary. Liberty and freedom were being sorely tested at this time. The world was in the grip of the Great Depression. In the United States, thousands of factories were closed and millions of workers had no jobs. In Asia, Japan was preparing to invade China. In Europe, Adolf Hitler of Germany and Benito Mussolini of Italy were in power. These two dictators were planning to snuff out liberty in Europe.

During the decade of the 1930s, just over half a million immigrants made their way to America. But more than 18 million had come during the first three decades of the century. "Here they found life because there was freedom to live," Roosevelt told the audience at Liberty's fiftieth birthday celebration. Among those who heard him was the grandson of Édouard-Réné Lefebvre de Laboulaye, the man whose dream led to the building of the Statue of Liberty.

The National Park Service had taken over the administration of the statue in 1933. Now, in 1937, it took control of the entire island. Plans were made to beautify the island and to repair parts of the statue. The island was closed to the public for about a year and a half. Some repair work was done, and in 1940 new mercury vapor lamps were installed. But when the United States entered World War II in December 1941, work on the statue was temporarily halted, and it was not completed until the 1950s. Liberty's lights were turned off during World War II, for fear of an enemy air raid. They were not turned on again until May 8, 1945—V-E (Victory in Europe) Day.

Hundreds of thousands of immigrants made their way to the United States in the years after World War II. Many of them were processed at Ellis Island. In half a century, more than 17 million immigrants passed through Ellis Island. In 1954, however, this way-station for immigrants was closed. In 1965 it was made part of the Statue of Liberty National Monument by President Lyndon B. Johnson.

At about the same time that Ellis Island was closed, the American Scenic and Historic Preservation Society proposed that a museum of immigration be built inside the pedestal of the Statue of Liberty. Work was begun on the museum in 1962 and was completed in 1972. The purpose of the museum is to show how millions of people from almost every other country on earth came to the United States and built a great nation—a nation dedicated to the ideal of liberty. The museum's displays show how the very first Americans—the Indians—came to America. They show how European immigrants made the journey by ship. They show something about most of the ethnic groups that make up the American people. There are maps and paintings, films and dioramas. There are even taped interviews with more than a hundred of the immigrants.

The museum has been a great success. Hundreds of thousands of people visited it during 1976, when the United States celebrated its bicentennial. Those who made the trip to Liberty Island to take part in America's two hundredth birthday also saw a special Bartholdi exhibition. The city of Colmar in France, where Bartholdi was born, has a Bartholdi Museum. It loaned a number of items to the National Park Service so they could be shown in the Bartholdi exhibition.

For the bicentennial, the Statue of Liberty also got a new lighting system. Sodium vapor lamps were put in the torch, and mercury vapor lamps were put in the crown. These lamps shined brightly during the bicentennial celebrations. One of the most beautiful sights was the dazzling fireworks display near Liberty Island.

1980s

In May of 1982, President Ronald Reagan announced the formation of a Statue of Liberty–Ellis Island Centennial Commission. This commission would raise money so that repairs could be made on the statue. Liberty was now almost one hundred years old, and she was beginning to show her age. The commission was also charged with renovating Ellis Island. The buildings there were run down, and vandals had caused even greater destruction. Finally, the commission was told to make plans for a great celebration of Lady Liberty's one hundredth birthday in 1986.

President Reagan named Lee Iacocca as head of the commission. When Iacocca, chairman of the Chrysler Corporation, accepted the chair of the Statue of Liberty–Ellis Island Centennial Commission, he said: "Our job now is to bring new life to these symbols of America's heritage. It is also our job to bring new life to the principles that sustained our parents and grandparents, and guided this country to greatness."

CHAPTER SIX

LIBERTY'S FACE-LIFT AND CENTENNIAL

 he Statue of Liberty–
Ellis Island Centennial
Commission immediately set out to raise money for Liberty's
restoration. Its nonprofit foundation was to do the work and
accept contributions. A number of major American corpora-
tions became official sponsors of the restoration work. But
much of the money was collected from individuals. When the
Statue of Liberty was built, French schoolchildren had contrib-
uted a lot of the money, and American schoolchildren had con-
tributed toward the cost of the pedestal. Now schoolchildren
once again showed their great interest in this most famous symbol of America. In schools throughout the country, fund-raising
drives were held. On their own, young people held fairs and
engaged in other activities to raise money for Lady Liberty.

The foundation estimated that it needed $230 million.
Restoration of the statue would cost $29 million. The cost of
administration, of fund raising, and of the various celebrations
would be another $43 million. And finally, $20 million was
needed to build an endowment to pay for future mainte-
nance.

THE DAMAGE DONE

The rest of the money collected by the Statue of Liberty–Ellis Island Foundation was earmarked for Ellis Island. This island, the gateway to America for 17 million immigrants, was in terrible shape. The grounds were overgrown by weeds. The dock had collapsed. Rain poured into the buildings through leaky roofs and broken windows. Worst of all, vandals had caused a great deal of destruction. Beautiful woodwork was destroyed. Huge chandeliers were smashed. Plumbing was ripped out. Desks and other furniture were smashed. The commission planned to spend about $138 million on Ellis Island. Most of the money was for restoration. But some of it was to be used to set up a computerized genealogy center. Here the sons and daughters of immigrants will be able to trace their families' histories. They will be able to find out the exact day their parents or grandparents came to the United States. They will be able to find out which ships they came on and which faraway cities they came from.

The National Park Service first discovered that Lady Liberty had problems in 1980. New lighting systems had been installed at various times. But other than that, very little major work had been done in almost a century. The Park Service found a number of problems. Some of them were structural, but others were caused by the salty air. And for the last twenty years, the statue has been pelted by acid rain and other forms of pollution. All of this took its toll on the statue.

Sectional view of Statue showing
spiral stairway and ladder to torch

*Damage such as this
is being repaired.*

The right arm and the torch that it holds were in very bad condition. Some of the damage was caused by Borglum, the person who redesigned the torch. Other damage was caused by an explosion in 1916 in an ammunition dump in nearby New Jersey. German saboteurs may have set off the explosion. The force of the blast popped some of the rivets in the statue. The connection between the right arm and the shoulder was badly weakened. In strong winds the arm moved as much as 15 inches (38 cm).

Other damage included a hole worn in the upraised arm by one of the spikes in Liberty's crown. Parts of her crown had crumbled—and pieces were found in the harbor. The frame of the observation deck was corroded, and the stairway to the crown was rusted. Handrails on the stairways were unsafe. Her gown was discolored and rust-spotted. And many of the two thousand iron straps that held the copper skin to the steel framework were corroded. Some of the rivets that held the straps to the skin and framework had popped out, allowing rainwater to seep in. Where this happened, there were rust spots.

REPAIR PLANS

French and American architectural engineers drew up plans to repair the statue, somewhat hampered by the fact that Eiffel's architectural plans of a century earlier had been destroyed in a fire. The engineers decided that rather than try to repair the torch, they would remove it and build a new one. The new one would be like Bartholdi's original—it would be solid and there would be no windows or glass. When Gutzon Borglum worked on the torch in 1916, he cut the windows in it. But the windows were not watertight. As a result, rainwater leaked into the torch, causing damage. Because there will be no lights or windows in

[51]

Repairs in progress

the new solid copper torch, it will be ringed with quartz-iodine lamps. These will shine on the torch, which will be gold plated as Bartholdi intended, creating the effect of a burning torch. The old torch will be placed in a museum in the basement of the Statue of Liberty.

Work began on the statue in January 1984. Workers put up three hundred tons of metal scaffolding around the statue, reaching from the base to the torch. Liberty Island will be kept open to the public, so visitors can watch the workers scampering about 300 feet (91 m) off the ground. Many visitors were present when, at a special ceremony, Liberty's torch was removed with a giant crane.

Work to be done includes repairing the spiral stairways, putting in rest areas, and installing a new emergency elevator to run from Liberty's foot to her shoulder. The enclosed elevator in Liberty's base will be replaced with a new hydraulic elevator. This elevator, which will be glass enclosed, will go only to the foot of the statue. Visitors will still have to climb hundreds of steps to get to the crown. For the comfort of these visitors, a new ventilation and air-conditioning system will be installed. The interior of the "old" Statue of Liberty could get uncomfortably hot during New York's humid summer months. Finally, the seams in Liberty's copper skin will be closed with a special sealant and the iron straps replaced—a few at a time—with special stainless steel bars. The interior will be completely cleaned of dirt and paint, so that visitors will be able to see the intricate steel framework and the ingenious method by which the entire statue is held together and supported.

GRAND FINALE

On July 4, 1986, more than three hundred modern ships and sailing ships will parade through Upper New York Bay. There

Above: *the torch being repaired*
Left: *Ms. Liberty encased in scaffolding*

will be fireworks displays and speeches. Bands will play the French and American national anthems. Guns will be fired in salute. The scene will be very much like the scene in 1886, when Auguste Bartholdi saw his dream come true—the unveiling of the Statue of Liberty.

Liberty will witness another ceremony on October 28, 1986. This will be the rededication ceremony—the day that Liberty is actually one hundred years old.

Liberty has stood in New York harbor for a century. Her upraised hand and torch have welcomed millions to America. She has given them hope. She has symbolized liberty and freedom. She has symbolized the United States. As David Moffitt, superintendent of the Statue of Liberty-Ellis Island National Monument, so aptly put it, "She means different things to different people—but they all have to do with what's good about this country."

Aerial view of Statue, looking up the Hudson River. The tall building at the top right is the Empire State Building.

CHAPTER SEVEN

FACTS AND FIGURES

NAMES

Copper Lady
Liberty Enlightening the World
Statue of Liberty
Miss Liberty
Ms. Liberty
Lady of Liberty
Lady with the Lamp
Mother of Exiles

LOCATION

Liberty Island (formerly Bedloe's Island)
in Upper New York Bay

WEIGHT

Steel framework—125 tons (113 MT)
Copper skin—100 tons (91 MT)
Total weight—225 tons (204 MT)

DIMENSIONS

Height of statue, from toe to torch
151 feet, 1 inch (46.05 m)

Height of pedestal and base
154 feet (46.96 m)

Total height
305 feet, 1 inch (92.99 m)

Height from head to toe
111 feet (33.83 m)

Head
17 feet, 3 inches (5.26 m) high

Nose
4 feet, 6 inches (1.37 m) long

Mouth
3 feet (91 cm) wide

Eye
2 feet, 6 inches (76 cm) wide

Waist
35 feet (10.67 m) thick

Right arm
42 feet (12.80 m) long

Left hand
16 feet, 5 inches (5.03 m) long

Index finger
8 feet (2.43 m) long

Fingernail
13 inches by 10 inches (33 cm × 25 cm)

Copper skin
3/32 of an inch (0.24 cm) thick

Tablet
23 feet, 7 inches by 13 feet, 7 inches (7.19 m × 4.14 m)

Crown
Seven spikes, or rays, representing the
seven seas and seven continents

CHRONOLOGY

1865

Édouard-Réné Lefebvre de Laboulaye, a French scholar,
proposes that a monument be built as a memorial to
American independence and French-American friendship.

1871
Auguste Bartholdi, a French sculptor and
friend of Laboulaye, proposes that a giant statue
—Liberty Enlightening the World—
be erected in New York harbor.

1875
Laboulaye organizes the Franco-American Union
to sponsor the statue and raise funds to build it;
Bartholdi builds his first model of the statue.

1876
The right arm and torch of the statue are displayed
in Philadelphia, at the Centennial Exposition.

1877
Bedloe's Island (now Liberty Island) is
selected as the site for the statue;
the American Committee for the Statue of Liberty
is formed to raise money for the statue's pedestal.

1878
Liberty's head is exhibited at the Paris World's Fair.

1881
The Franco-American Union raises enough money
to build the statue.

1883
Emma Lazarus writes the poem "The New Colossus"
to help raise funds for the pedestal; work on
the pedestal begins.

1884
The statue is completed and officially presented to
the United States at a special ceremony in Paris;
the cornerstone of the pedestal is laid.

1885
The Statue of Liberty arrives in New York;
Joseph Pulitzer and his newspaper, *The World*,
campaign for funds for the pedestal.

1886
The pedestal is completed in April;
the Statue of Liberty is unveiled on October 28.

1902
The Statue of Liberty is placed under
the jurisdiction of the War Department.

1903
Emma Lazarus's poem is inscribed on a tablet
and placed on the statue's pedestal.

1916
A new lighting system is installed.

1924
The Statue of Liberty is declared a national monument.

1931
A new floodlighting system is installed.

1933
The Statue of Liberty is placed under the jurisdiction
of the National Park Service.

1936
President Franklin D. Roosevelt presides over ceremonies
to celebrate the Statue of Liberty's fiftieth birthday.

1956
Bedloe's Island is renamed Liberty Island;
it is announced that an American Museum of Immigration
will be built in the base of the statue.

1965
Ellis Island is made part of
the Statue of Liberty National Monument.

1972
The American Museum of Immigration is
completed and opened to the public.

1976
The Bartholdi Exhibit opens during
the celebration of America's bicentennial.

1982
President Ronald Reagan announces the
formation of the Statue of Liberty–
Ellis Island Centennial Commission.

1984
Work begins on refurbishing the Statue of Liberty
for the statue's 1986 centennial.

1986
Special celebrations are held to commemorate
the Statue of Liberty's one hundredth birthday.

INDEX